FOUR PILLARS OF WISDOM
A Grandmother's Love

DA'RON COX

AuthorHouse™
1663 Liberty Drive
Bloomington, IN 47403
www.authorhouse.com
Phone: 833-262-8899

Because of the dynamic nature of the Internet, any web addresses or links contained in this book may have changed
since publication and may no longer be valid. The views expressed in this work are solely those of the author and do
not necessarily reflect the views of the publisher, and the publisher hereby disclaims any responsibility for them.

Any people depicted in stock imagery provided by Getty Images are models,
and such images are being used for illustrative purposes only.
Certain stock imagery © Getty Images.

This book is printed on acid-free paper.

ISBN: 979-8-8230-3101-1 (sc)
       979-8-8230-3103-5 (hc)
       979-8-8230-3102-8 (e)

Library of Congress Control Number: 2024916225

Print information available on the last page.

Published by AuthorHouse 09/23/2024

authorHOUSE®

Dedicated to my nephew,

DALC

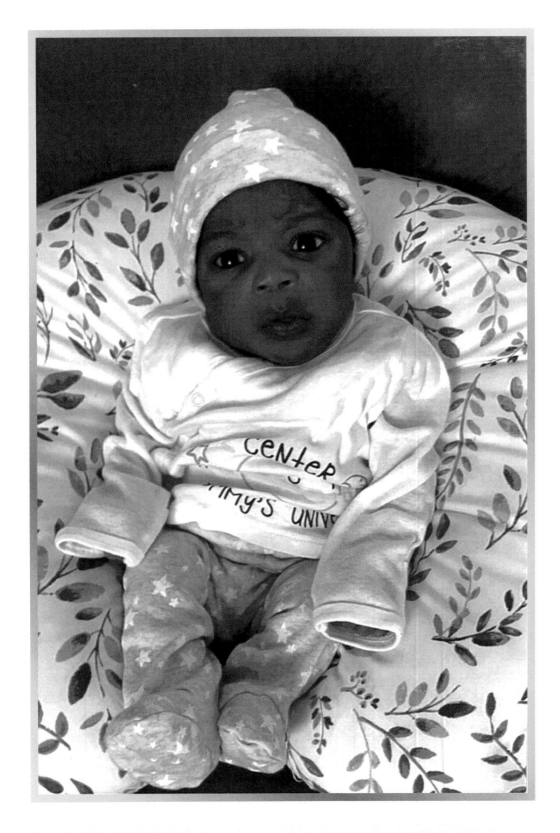

TABLE OF CONTENTS

FOREWORD

This a curious distinction for me. Originally, the song lyrics for Makaveli's "White Man'z World" were supposed to occupy this space, but getting permission to use them would have required more red tape than a crime scene. So Da'Ron asked me if I wouldn't mind opening his book for him. Although Da'Ron and I have known each other for over a decade here on the inside, I was of the mind that the honor should go to someone who held a more significant role in his life. But he felt I knew him well enough, and I for sure knew his book, because I edited and typed it up and was consulted on virtually every aspect of it. So, as far as he was concerned, I was ideally suited to have this little chat with y'all. That is, if I *wanted* to do it.

Yes, that was a guilt trip you just read. Now let me tell you why it worked.

When Da'Ron and I first hooked up, it was from him inviting me into a business venture of his. We made a nice bit of change together, and I will say this for my part of it: I made money faster than I could spend it. Real rap. And it was through that interaction, the need of our reliance on each other during that venture, that a friendship developed. We came to the mutual understanding that we were principled in our dealings with one another—honest and equitable. Convicts who are standup are a dying breed in these camps, so when we come across each other, we tend to close ranks. As such, when a favor is asked between us, it's never done lightly. And besides, I do know the worth of the words in this book better than most.

I tell you, as a professional writer myself, that to do what Brother Da'Ron has done here required self-sacrifice. He bled to give you what you have in your hands. And believe me, there was a lot more blood involved until heads wiser than ours came to stanch the flow, to make sure he held just enough in reserve to keep himself from perishing, so to speak.

Da'Ron's story is an uncommon one. If you are expecting a typical "tale from the hood," all about drug deals gone wrong and body bags, yeah, that's not what this is. But for those of you of a younger generation— especially you young brothers and sisters eager to be someone of substance, in character and wealth—there is instruction here for you. Da'Ron has taken on the mantle of an elder, the kind so many of whom are presently confined to concrete cages by a system whose racially biased motivations have become more evident to an increasingly woke populace. And whether you are young or old, on the inside or out, it is in that capacity that he provides the hope Tupac so desperately expressed to carry us to better times in this white man'z world.

Vaughn Wright
SCI Huntingdon
September 2023

INTRODUCTION

Don't let good get in the way of great!

—Puma

My name is Da'Ron Albert Lee Cox, a.k.a. Chiccen. At the age of three, my maternal grandmother, Evelyn Cox, a.k.a. Grams, taught me her four pillars of wisdom to prepare me for what I would face in the world as a *Black man*. She would go on to explain that I had two things working against me from conception to inception through no fault of my own. I was *Black*, and one day I would grow up to be a *man*. Statistically I was doomed. Grams was determined to equip me with the necessary spiritual, mental, and emotional tools to succeed in spite of what was awaiting me. A system that was established for me to fail!

I was taught not to allow what others thought of me to deter me from being the best person I could be. My grams explained that to be successful as a *Black man* in America, I must work twice as hard and be three times smarter than everyone else. Education is key in getting ahead in life; I must have drive and determination, because as a *Black man*, I am likely to encounter more noes than yesses in my pursuit of success.

Never allow that stop you. Education is the first step in mastering math, religion, and politics, for they represent the cornerstones of the world. There are four pillars that make up the foundation for a *Black man* to build upon to create his place in the world.

Education is a tool used to create an advantage in whatever dream you aspire to in life. Math is a tool used to solve problems in life and to help you understand the value and workings of money. Religion is a source of truth, guidance, faith, hope, and comfort for one's life—the way in which God intended for us to live life, abundantly blessed. Politics is how one is perceived in the eyes of others and how to form relationships.

I intend to share my gram's wisdom through the pages of this book and explain how her wisdom impacted my life. It was my grandmother who taught me how to conduct myself as a *man*, and how to present myself as a *Black man*. To be proud of who I am with confidence. To have self-respect, self-love, and self-worth. To truly know and understand I have a purpose and a place in this world too!

PILLAR I EDUCATION

Education is the ultimate equalizer. It doesn't matter what your socioeconomic status is. If you've got education, you have power.

—Marilyn Booker

All education, all knowledge, is cumulative and builds personal power.

—Hill Harper

Education starts with the knowledge of yourself, your history, and your ancestors. Having such knowledge provides you with a sense of pride, strength, confidence, and self-respect that no one can take from you. This is one's cornerstone of consciousness; no one can tell you otherwise of your worth and purpose.

Aristotle said, "The roots of education are bitter, but the fruit is sweet," which speaks to the journey of how the Black man came to receive an education in America. The Black man's journey regarding education has always been an uphill battle. It started out as being illegal for us to learn how to read or write as slaves. The slave masters felt we would not be fit to be slaves if we knew how to read or write. There would be no keeping us. The slave masters knew being able to read and write really meant equality—and the path to freedom.

A Black man's education seems to come by way of improvisation or forced by law. There was *Brown v. Board of Education* and affirmative action, which meant to include us and provide a level and fair playing field for us to thrive. But it was only met with mobs of hate, as the educators imposed their prejudices upon us by showing and expressing how we didn't belong in their schools. As if the color of our skin was contagious and carried some type of low-aptitude herpes.

What was supposed to be given to us as a right has always been presented as a privilege that can be taken away. This was a tactic used to keep us in a place of inferiority.

As Grams shared her four pillars of wisdom with me when I was three years old, she set up a makeshift school for me. This was the beginning of the life lessons and path she was creating for me to be able to succeed in life. She taught me math and how to read and write. When teaching me to read, she would record me with my Fisher-Price tape recorder. She would then play it back so I could hear myself read. She would help me sound out the words I had trouble with until I pronounced them correctly.

Once reading was completed, we moved on to math. She made flash cards of numbers, both addition and subtraction problems. The flash cards went one through ten, eleven through twenty, and so on. When I would get stuck with a problem, she would say, "Use your fingers," and then demonstrate by using her own fingers to show me. Next, I would practice writing the alphabet, numbers, my name, address, and phone number. My grams would use the paper that allowed children to trace letters and numbers so that I could learn to write capital letters, lower-case letters, and numbers. We would do this daily for hours. She also used puzzles to help me with my memory, including picture cards that I had to match to make a pair.

As I got older, Grams would take me to art festivals and museums to learn about different cultures. She would say, "I am raising you to be particular, not to think you are better than anyone." This was my introduction to the Golden Rule: "Treat people the way you would like to be treated." Grams wanted me to know and understand who I was and my history. She gave me books to read about the many great accomplishments and contributions made by Black people, the Reconstruction era, the Attica riot, Donald Goines, and Iceberg Slim. Grams had a way in teaching me. She would cook a dish we never had before or make my favorite snack. We would then sit down and watch documentaries such as *Eyes on the Prize*, films on the march on Washington and the riots, and the movie *Roots*. It wasn't enough to read the book or watch the documentaries and movies; she wanted to know what I thought, felt, and got out of them all. We would exchange questions and answers. Grams did her best to answer all my questions and at times would steer me in the direction to find the answer myself.

My grams wanted me to see as many pictures as possible of how the world would see me as a Black man—right, wrong, good, or bad. It was up to me to change the perception for myself and choose how I wanted to be perceived as a person and a Black man. Through education we become prepared for our responsibilities in life.

School came easy to me because I enjoyed learning new things and the challenge of solving problems. I squandered a great deal of opportunities where my education was concerned. Both Moms and Grams made sacrifices for me to have options of opportunities in life. They made a way for me to attend Greater Works Christian Academy, a private school in Murrysville, Pennsylvania, as a freshman.

I say "made a way," because at the time my family didn't own a car. They felt my education was more important. I lived in Homewood-Brushton, Pennsylvania, which is some distance from Murrysville. If I missed the school bus due to a weather delay, I had to catch a jitney to school. I would use this as an excuse not to go to school. I wasted Moms's and Grams's money, as well as my opportunity, by failing the ninth grade for missing too many days of school.

While attending Greater Works Christian Academy, I was a member of the Ketchum Junior Advertising Program, where I learned how to create ads for companies. I had an opportunity to work on an ad campaign for Ford Motors. The program was held at the PPG Building in Market Square in downtown Pittsburgh.

During my sophomore year at Westinghouse High School, which is in Homewood-Brushton, Pennsylvania, I was a member of the Young Entrepreneur Program, which was held at Pitt University. The program taught us about the characteristic traits that made up an entrepreneur, how to start and build a successful business, and, most importantly, how to manage money. They gave us money to open checking and savings accounts. This program was amazing in every way. They had business fairs, where entrepreneurs would come speak and give personal accounts of their journey in business, their successes and failures, and their drive and determination to build a successful business not only for themselves but for their families and communities.

The direction of my life shifted when I decided to chase triple-beam dreams with a pocketful of stones, trying to get that illusive million while I was young. I abandoned my sport of choice, which was baseball, to slang cocaine. Baseball came natural to me from the time I picked up a bat and put on a uniform at the age of seven for the Homewood Pirates Little League baseball team. I fell in love with the game.

During my junior year of high school, the baseball coach at Westinghouse recruited me to play for the team. He promised me that if I played for him and kept my grades right, he would do everything he could to get me a full scholarship to go to college. This is how much he believed in me. He just asked that I trust him to have my best interests in mind. I went to one practice. It felt great. Both coach and I were excited.

It's not that I didn't trust coach to have my best interests in mind, but after my first practice, I bought my first four-and-a-half ounces of cocaine. I had aspirations of playing a different game. Instead of chasing a free education and a chance to make millions, I chose to chase thousands and a ten- to twenty-year prison sentence. That's what happens when you think small: you end up settling!

Big Momma sat me down my junior year as well, asking what my plans were for college. I had aspirations of attending Norfolk State and majoring in international business. She told me not to worry about the cost; she would pay for it. Going as far as signing me up, she paid for me to take SAT prep classes and drove me and her daughter to and from classes with breakfast from McDonald's, so I would be prepared to take the SAT exam.

I was an honor-roll student when I attended school. It was my after-school activities that were an issue. I told myself if I did well in school, I could do what I wanted outside of school.

I am from 707 Fleury Way Way. Doing what I wanted meant I could be found on Fleury Way in the "trap." I straddled the fence well, or at least that's what I told myself between serving fiends while doing homework and going to school straight from the alley after pulling all-nighters.

Grams was not a fan of my hustling endeavors. She forbade me to bring drugs or money that was made from selling drugs into her house. What did I do? I brought them both into her house. Very disrespectful on my part. She told me stories of her husband and his drug exploits bringing money into her house, and how she sent both him and his money right back out the front door. Here I was repeating the same act that she believed ruined her family.

I remember Grams found a quart bottle of uncut formaldehyde in my bedroom. She told me to get that mess out of her house. I asked her why she was in my bedroom in the first place, and in the garbage, no less. I thought I was doing something slick by hiding the bottle in the trash can, thinking she wouldn't know what it was. Well, she knew exactly what it was. She reminded me that she paid the bills in the house and that was her bedroom, not mine! I was just a guest, more or less.

One day I had a sale for the formaldehyde and went to Grams's house to retrieve the bottle, only to find that she had thrown the bottle away. I asked, "Grams, where's that bottle at?"

She said, "I told you to get that out of my house."

I replied, "You threw away ten thousand dollars. You don't know if I owe someone that money or not."

She said, "You should have thought about that when I told you the first time to get it out of my house." I didn't owe anyone, but that was a loss I couldn't afford. I was way out of line breaking the cardinal rule: never stash drugs where you lay your head or in Grams's or Moms's house.

Selling drugs was a rollercoaster for me. I tried to play both sides, school and trappin'. There is a false perception that fast money will always be available, so you blow it just as fast as you make it. I learned I wasn't making nearly as much money as I thought. I was offered a storefront with a fully equipped, working kitchen, with three apartments on top of the storefront, for $50,000. I didn't have the money to capitalize on the opportunity.

In chasing the spoils of selling drugs, I subjected myself to the consequences that come with that lifestyle. No, I wasn't a cowboy, but I was active. Losing my life in the manner that I have, I how much how much money I lost in chasing a drug dealer's dream, instead of how much money I made.

I think about the time I have been incarcerated and what I could have accomplished. I use McDonald's as an example.

McDonald's is just a job many don't want or see any real opportunity in, but that depends on your vision and your endgame. Say I got hired at McDonald's when I was eighteen. I could have worked my way into management by the age of twenty or twenty-one. I would have used that opportunity to position myself to own a McDonald's franchise(s) with the assistance of the company's financing by the age of twenty-five or twenty-six. Instead of checcin' for Calvin, I looked up to the G'z and hustlers, knowing exactly what awaited me by choosing the left side, and more than willing to accept the inevitable outcome of my demise. Homewood could have used a McDonald's. I know it's easier said than done. The question becomes, are you willing to do what you have never done to have what you never had?

Due to failing the ninth grade, I had to attend both summer and night school to make up credits to graduate from high school. I was determined to graduate. It wasn't just for me or about me. Many people had invested time and resources for me to succeed; to see me graduate would have been a return on their investment.

Instead, I was arrested and found guilty of a homicide, sentenced to life without parole, plus three and a half to seven years for a violation of the Uniform Firearms Act. At the time of my arrest, I was a senior attending Westinghouse High School. I was arrested in January 1997, was due to graduate in June 1997, and was found guilty in July 1997. One hell of a trifecta without a winner.

Even while I was incarcerated, I continued to pursue an education, receiving my GED in December 1997. Today I strive to be the best version of myself, putting myself in a position to succeed despite my circumstances. Grams told me, "Your body is locked, up, son, but not your mind."

When I first made it upstate, a man named Latif took me under his wing. He showed me how to navigate the perils of incarceration, explaining that I had two objectives while serving my time. The first objective was to get out of jail by learning my case inside out, understanding that no one should know my case better than me. He taught me how to research case law and how to file legal paperwork such as postconviction motions, briefs, and amended petitions.

My second objective was to put myself in a position to be considered for another chance at life if the law so happened to change. This required me to focus on life beyond incarceration. I went to school and worked on my case day in and day out, researching cases and the law pertaining to my case. Nothing else mattered! I participated in programs that allowed me to work on the skills necessary to achieve success post incarceration.

Homewood Ave.

I went on to complete two correspondence courses in small business management and real estate appraisal, picking up a few trades to receive certifications in vinyl siding and from the National Center for Construction, Education and Research. I also became a facilitator for the Fathers' Initiative Program of America. As a nineteen-year-old boy, I had a lot to learn about myself and what I wanted out of my life. Latif helped me with that. He taught me that one's life is not determined nor defined by what someone else thinks, but by the determination and drive of the individual who wants better for himself. He would tell me that I have my whole life ahead of me, and I was to make the best use of this time to prepare for the life I wanted to live.

Education is an ongoing process and a necessity in one's life. The value of knowledge is to use it. Understanding knowledge and experience is invaluable. Carter G. Woodson said, "Real education means to inspire people to live more abundantly, to learn to begin with life as they find it and make it better."

It's not enough that our schools lag in reading, math, and science. Now they want to take away the opportunity for us to learn about who we are, the trauma caused by slavery and redlining, and what part we contributed to the great nation of the United States of America.

To date, there has been legislation passed in fourteen states and introduced in at least twenty-one others to limit or outright ban the teaching of African American history. These states label such teachings as a divisive concept. The reason behind this so-called legislation is because the powers that be don't want the descendants of those who have oppressed an entire race, implementing the systemic disadvantages placed upon said race—African Americans—to bear the burdens of the actions of their forefathers.

The state of Florida seems to be leading the charge with its anti-woke campaign, championed by the guidance of Governor Ron DeSantis, who said, and I quote, "Black people benefited from slavery." As if Black people have a great deal to be thankful for, for being captured, beaten, raped, and tortured mentally and physically, while being transported to a foreign land to work against our will.

This has played a major role in the mental health crisis suffered for generations in our communities, and at times has given way to a subservient disposition in how we see ourselves and carry ourselves as a people.

Always seek knowledge, stay current or run the risk of being left behind.
This is why education should never be taken for granted.
There was a time our people would risk death to have any form of education.
Let's honor them by making sure our history is taught for generations to come.

Brushton Ave.

To know wisdom and instruction, to perceive the words of understanding, to receive the instruction of wisdom, justice, judgement, and equity; to give prudence to the simple, to the young man knowledge and discretion—a wise man will hear and increase learning, and a man of understanding will attain wise counsel, to understand a proverb and an enigma, the words of the wise and their riddles. The fear of the Lord is the beginning of knowledge, but fools despise wisdom and instruction.

—Proverbs 1:2–7

PILLAR II MATH

Mistakes will be made, trial and error will happen, forging a new path is likely to result in hitting several dead ends before success is met. Planning provides a framework for success, not a direct line. Obstacles always come, and we need to be aware (even anticipate) that setbacks will occur.

—Hill Harper

Math

Life is a contest between you and yourself.

—Mark Twain

Math serves dual purposes. In no specific order, math serves as a way of solving life problems and understanding the world of finances. Life is full of surprises, and all surprises are not welcome. How does one face obstacles and adversities? More often than not, one will react mainly from a negative emotion triggered by fear, going straight into defense mode or self-preservation, instead of taking a step back and looking into the full scale of what the obstacle or adversity entails. In turn, one will end up making a bad decision without taking into account the consequences or, worse yet, not caring about any consequences at all. This very thought process limits your thinking and actions, which boxes you into a corner that compromises your self-preservation. I was advised never to react out of anger or despair. Instead, always strive to collect yourself first, your thoughts, and keep everything in front of you. This will allow you to make a sound decision, stopping you from doing something you cannot come back from.

John Milton wrote in *Paradise Lost*, "The mind is its own place, and in itself can make a Heaven of Hell, a Hell of Heaven." Take the time to think ... then react. In *The 7 Habits of Highly Effective People*, the author describes a paradigm that consists of a win-win, lose-win, win-lose, and a lose-lose situation. What I came to gather from the paradigm was that there may come a time you have to lose in order to win. You must avoid a lose-lose situation at all costs. This requires a big-picture thinker whose pride is not controlled by what the outside non-factors have to say. Nothing from nothing equals nothing. You have to be careful with a win-lose scenario, because that can be detrimental and costly in the end. What you lose can be more valuable than what you win. In a perfect world, we all would like a win-win situation. It happens more than we acknowledge. It's not always about you. Do a selfless act by extending a hand that helps someone get through a tough time or exchange of a kind word. You never know the impact you can have on a person's day or life when you don't worry about what's in it for you.

Before my life was abruptly uprooted on January 14, 1997, I had three conversations that turned out to be paramount. If only I had taken heed. Three very important women had separate conversations with me regarding my state of mental and emotional well-being.

I had Thanksgiving dinner with Big Momma and my extended family. I was in a relationship with Big Momma's youngest daughter. As the night came to an end, Mama Tee took me home. Unbeknownst to me, the conversation I would have with her would be the first of three significant talks I would have leading up to the very weekend before my last day of freedom.

Mama Tee and I sat in the car in front of Grams's house for about thirty minutes. It was a very deep and personal discussion about what she had overcome in her life, how blessed she felt to be with the love of her life and to be in the presence of family. She couldn't see that for herself at one time in her life, she shared with me. Then the conversation took a turn.

She said, "I don't know the extent of what's going on with you or what you're into, but the family is worried." She then suggested that I take a step back and take inventory of my life, and expressed how much the family loved me and cared about me. Then she hit a sore spot for me and brought up my girlfriend, saying much she loved me and what a good girl she was. At the time, I was neglecting my relationship and taking my girl for granted. Mama Tee let me know I could lose everything over nothing. One of many lose-lose situations.

I didn't know how to respond. As I was caught up in my thoughts, Mama Tee ended the conversation. We said our goodbyes and I love yous.

Two weeks later, my girlfriend was over my house helping me with my Spanish homework. She spoke Spanish very well. When we were done and I had a better understanding of the Spanish language, she called Big Momma to come pick her up. After I walked her to the car, I knelt down to greet Big Momma through the passenger window. She asked what was going on with me. I said not much. Her response was, "I doubt that." I asked her what that meant. She said, "I know you are in over your head. You need to think about what's going on in your life."

Big Momma had reason to be concerned. At the time, the neighborhood feuds were peaking and spilled over into school. There was a lot going on, heat everywhere, no place was safe. I caught jitneys to and from school, or my lady friend dropped me off, not to get caught slippin' walking home. By chance, when I did walk home, I had to be heavy, hittin' every cut and alley from Monticello Street to Fleury Way, Frankstown Avenue and Bennett Street being the only open streets I had to cross. Once I hit Fleury Way by Bethesda Church, I felt safe, because I was in my alley.

That wasn't always the case. There were nights I caught jitneys from Fleury Way to Kelly Street because I may have had an eerie feeling someone was lurkin' in the cut, waiting for one of us to walk through to down us. The jitney drivers didn't understand, nor did they care, as long as they got paid. The way I saw it, the two dollars it cost to drive me around the corner was well worth saving my life.

Big Momma's whole thing was that I needed to put things into perspective before it got too late. "I hear you," I replied.

She said, "Do you?" Then she asked where I was going. I told her I had to go to Fleury Way for a minute. She caught an instant attitude. The conversation we just had was about backing up from the alley. Big Momma just shook her head and pulled off, no goodbye. That's how I knew she was disappointed in me.

What Big Momma didn't know was that although I was hustling on Fleury Way, I also had a woman who lived in the alley. This was the second conversation of the three.

Friday, January 9, 1997, after school, I was in my room at Grams's house, watching Looney Tunes and eating a snack, decompressing. My grams came home from work, asked how I was doing and how my day was. I told her I was cool, and school went well. She, in turn, suggested I stay in for the night without drinking, smoking weed, listening to music, or having any company. "Take some time for yourself," she said. "Think about what's going on around you, where you are, and where you're going." Taken aback, I told Grams I was cool, and she said, "You are the coolest, most confused individual I know," before shutting my bedroom door.

Not even two minutes later she came back with an attitude, and told me I needed God, Jesus, Allah, or Buddha, because I needed help. I'm like, "Grams, I'm cool."

And she said, "No, you're not. Bad part is you can't see that." I just left the house for the night.

It was Friday night, and what did I do? I got a bottle of Seagram's gin and some fire weed, then went over a friend's house. She was home from college for the holidays, and I wanted to spend some time with her before she went back. I spent a few hours with her. I ended my night by going over to my daughter's mother's house in Point Breeze.

I woke up Saturday morning and attended to my daughter, holding her, looking into her innocent eyes. Her moms and I picked back up with a conversation that started the night before about us becoming a family. I must admit, I wasn't ready for that responsibility and commitment. It was weighing heavy on me. I left that conversation to be continued.

I called a jitney, and before I went home, I told the driver to go to the Lincoln Cemetery so I could have a drink and talk with my big bro from 707 Fleury Way (70ve). I still had the bottle of gin. I poured a shot on his tombstone and took a shot. It was the dead of winter at nine-thirty in the morning. After about twenty minutes of talking and trading shots, I got back into the waiting jitney and told the driver to take me to Kelly Street.

Along the way, I could see the driver was a bit uneasy, looking for a way to say something after watching me have a conversation with a tombstone for nearly half an hour, exchanging drinks. Not wanting to be intrusive, he just asked if I was all right. I told him I was cool. We rode in silence after that. I'm sure he was happy to get me out of his car.

Saturday nights were reserved for date nights with a lady friend I was courting at the time. That Saturday nothing worthwhile was playing at the movie theater, so we went to dinner and then back to my house to watch a movie and enjoy each other's company.

Sunday, I visited the home of my big bro, the one I had spent Saturday morning with at the cemetery. I spent Sundays with his son and his son's moms. I would play video games with his son and watch the Steelers games with his moms. I really enjoyed that time with them.

Wednesday, January 14, 1997, I received a 911 page from Moms. I called back immediately. She answered in a state of hysteria. As I was telling her to calm down, she was crying, saying there was a warrant out for my arrest. The police believed I was armed and dangerous.

Taken aback, I asked what she was talking about. The police had gone to Moms's apartment building looking for me, but they had gone to the wrong apartment, showing someone else's picture and asking for me. Moms, scared out of her mind, asked me to turn myself in. I asked why I would when I didn't know what for. She asked me if I was going to let the police kick my grams's door in. "The police think you have a gun and will use it if you cross paths with them." Moms thought the police would shoot me on sight. I was high on 'noid, thinking of all types of scenarios of how things could play out. What's my move?

I told Moms to come pick me up from Brushton Avenue. I did everything not to turn myself in. I was trying to sober up, to get my mind right. Nothing I did made sense. I had Moms stop at Baker's and then Hoagie Castle. Each time I was thinking of hittin' a cut, running to one of my homies' or homegirls' houses, calling Moms later to explain why I couldn't turn myself in. She realized what I was doing and pulled over. She said, "Please turn yourself in. I don't want to lose you."

I turned myself in.

It's been twenty-six years since I have been home. I was told to take a step back, collect myself and my thoughts and put some order into my life. I didn't take heed. For years, Moms felt at fault for asking me to turn myself in. I absolved her of that burden. She thought she was protecting me from the police killing me *cold* in the streets!

This is a lose-win scenario when you are an individual who can get up after being knocked down. Ever since, I have not been defined by what happened, but by what I made from what has happened.

No man can express himself in terms of opulence while most of
his thought-power is given over to the maintenance of a poverty consciousness.

—Anonymous

Math Deux

You don't know my struggle, so you can't feel my hustle.

—Boosie

Grams would say you can't plant corn and expect to grow tomatoes, or you can't have steak taste with baked-bean money. She wasn't wasteful with money and didn't live beyond her means. She struggled a day or two in her life while raising three children in a two-bedroom apartment in the Hill District's Robinson Court Housing Projects. During this time, she would do people's hair in the kitchen, dead people's hair at a funeral home, wash cars, and clean houses.

Grams flipped out when her husband signed her up for welfare. She had to figure out what she was going to do. The last thing she wanted to do or be on was welfare. She looked at it as a way for her husband to control her. She refused to be controlled by her husband or the government.

One day she up and left, leaving her three children in the apartment by themselves. She went to Ohio to get her mind right. She was gone for a week, and no one knew where she was or if she was coming back.

When she did return from her retreat of sorts, a friend of hers told her about a school security guard job that had opened up at the board of education. She applied and was hired. When her children came home from school one day, the apartment was packed up and they moved to Homewood-Brushton, Pennsylvania. Life changed for Grams and her children from that day. Grams never lived beyond her means and was OK living right at the cusp of her means; that way she was comfortable but not struggling.

Grams believed in having two streams of income, a primary job and a hustle. She worked as a school security guard for the board of education for thirty-plus years, which was her primary job. At one point, she worked at Gabby's barbershop on Homewood Avenue. Then she worked at Shakespeare Giant Eagle in the seafood and deli departments for twenty-plus years. The barbershop and Giant Eagle jobs served as her hustles, along with sidewalk sales in front of the house. She occasionally cleaned people's houses on her off days too.

Grams explained that the money you made from your primary job was the money used to pay your bills and to save. The money you made from your hustles was used for groceries, outings, clothing, and so forth. Your credit was used for big expenses, but only if you could handle the payments. She always paid her bills a month in advance, never wanting to be behind. It was a fear from the days of old.

One of the things I learned about money included how to balance a checkbook, which added to my lessons in math. I would balance the checkbook by subtracting the amount I wrote the check for from the most recently dated balance in the checkbook. I would practice writing and signing checks. I had a signature before I knew how to write in cursive. I copied how Grams signed her name on the check. I still sign my name the same way I learned at four years old.

My introduction to earning my own money came by way of chores: cleaning my room and the bathroom, taking out the trash, and shoveling snow. My first job was a paper route. I was nine years old, but Grams told the man she would help me. I delivered the daily, evening, and Sunday Pittsburgh *Post-Gazette*.

I lived on Kelly Street, and my paper route was from Idlewild Street to Kedron Street. Grams and I rolled the papers to be delivered before she went to her second job. On Sundays, we used a City Foods shopping cart to deliver Sunday papers.

I will never forget how, in the middle of the 1987 winter blizzard, we pushed that shopping cart delivering Sunday papers. We had a garbage bag over the cart so the papers wouldn't get wet. Of course, that only helped for a moment. We were selling papers to people going to church and stuck in the snow. They were paying five and ten dollars a paper. They felt bad for us. We delivered every paper. Grams told me I had a job to do, and the weather was not an excuse not to get it done. People paid their money for my service.

Grams used my paper route to plant the seed and explanation of the importance of saving money. She nurtured and cultivated that seed by also teaching me how to shop and get the most for my money. I had my last Christmas at the age of ten. From the age of eleven, I was given money to catch the day-after-Christmas and New Year's sales to get twice, and sometimes three times, more than I would have if I woke up to gifts under a tree for Christmas.

I would shop for clothes in off seasons, buying winter pieces in the summer and summer pieces in the fall and winter. I would buy pieces that didn't go out of style and add to them the season's new line, allowing me to fall in on trend on a budget.

My second job was cleaning and running errands at Wade's Beauty Salon on Kelly Street, making fifteen dollars a week plus tips. If I saved ten dollars of the fifteen dollars I made, Grams would add fifteen dollars to it, giving me twenty-five dollars, which I would save weekly. This was her way of giving me an incentive to save money. My third job was working at the miniature golf course on Frankstown Avenue.

Learning the value of a dollar and understanding the importance of saving money, I was taught that no one was going to give me money without me working for it. From chores, shoveling snow, delivering papers, sweeping up hair, carrying bags to cars at Giant Eagle, selling bootleg tapes on Homewood Avenue, and working at the miniature golf course, I got to a dollar. Although I had a knack for making a dollar and saving a dollar, I had no idea how to make my money work for me.

As I furthered my understanding about money, I learned how to make the money I worked for work for me. Grams had a formula of two streams of income: your job and your hustle. I prefer three streams of income: your job, your hustle, and your investments. You work your job and your hustle, while your investments work for you.

I was eleven years old when I was introduced to the stock market through an infomercial at three in the morning about the *Wall Street Journal*. The tagline was, "If you want to make money, get a subscription to the *Wall Street Journal*. It will teach you about the financial markets and how to make money." I ordered a year's subscription. I had no idea what financial markets were; neither did Grams, and she had paid for the subscription. I had to learn. Grams sought a mentor for me from the PNC Bank on Homewood Avenue to help me understand the world of investing. It wasn't until I was incarcerated that I made my first investment in the stock market. I bought four shares and a fractional share of Walmart through a dividend reinvestment program (DRIP). You can reinvest the dividends paid to you by the company or receive the dividends as payments while your stocks continue to grow.

It was 1999, and this was a stone-age approach to investing. I had to write Walmart for an application to make my initial investment through their DRIP program. This was a step in the right direction to have my money work for me. The greatest lesson I learned in making the investment was that I didn't need a lot of money. I made my initial investment with $120.

Since then, I have devised a portfolio of investments that was acquired with minimum investments of fifty dollars to $1,000. I look for value stocks and electronic traded funds (ETFs) to invest in, getting the most for my dollars and cents. I also invest in silver and gold coins, learning the value in buying and selling coins. There are three factors in dealing with coins: 1) condition; 2) rarity; and 3) metal (silver or gold).

I read in a *Bloomberg Weekly* article that homeownership is the main way American families accumulate wealth. There is a gap between Black homeownership and white homeownership. At the height of the COVID pandemic, homeownership among Black Americans was 45 percent, compared with 67.4 percent for all US households, and 75 percent for white people, according to US Census Bureau data.

In learning this information, it made me seek the best path to accumulate wealth. I came across an article in *USA Today* that provided a chart of ways to become wealthy. Sure enough, real estate was the front-runner.

USA Today "Snapshot: How to Become Wealthy":

19 percent invest in real estate
15 percent get a professional degree
14 percent inherit money
13 percent invest in stocks or mutual funds
12 percent start a business

I've been engrossed in learning how to invest in real estate, the financial markets, and starting my own company. I'm striving to create a unicorn, which is a company evaluated to be worth a billion dollars or more. I am very encouraged with all that is available to achieve my goals from Robinhood Inc., Stash, We Bull, Schwab Slices, and Acorns that assist me to make investments with as little as five dollars and spare change. SimpliFi, Chime, Self, and SoFi will help me get my credit right. These financial tools will help me budget to save money, put me in position to fund my aspirations with my money or other people's money (due to my great credit score) in real estate and financial markets and to create a unicorn from an idea I conjured up to be of service to my people.

Money is a mentality created out of habit. You either have a poor person's mentality with poor money habits, or a rich person's mentality with an understanding of money with good money habits. It is said, "Poor people talk about money, rich people talk about material things, and wealthy people talk about ideas!" Which is why 84 percent of equity wealth in this country is owned by 10 percent of the wealthiest people.

There is federal data that shows, as of 2023, the top 1 percent of American earners now control more wealth than the nation's entire middle class combined. The top 1 percent hold $38.7 trillion in wealth. They accomplished this by being in position to take advantage of and capitalize off down times such as the Great Recession and the COVID-19 pandemic, which created the low-interest years when stocks and housing prices soared. If you owned homes, stocks, and retirement accounts, more than likely you did very well for yourself.

Being we as a people lack home and stock ownership, we missed out on taking advantage of refinancing at lower interest rates and buying more stocks at bargain prices, getting both quality and quantity investments for our money. What I find most fascinating is that the 1 percent made their fortunes through businesses such as auto dealerships, beverage distribution, and owning multiple franchises. These 1 percenters are referred to as low-profile multimillionaires. They don't have the notoriety of an Elon Musk, so to speak, being that he's a billionaire. However, they represent us and what is attainable through grind and determination. The 1 percent control more than 12.9 percent of the real estate wealth, hold close to half of all corporate equities and mutual fund shares, and nearly half of all private company wealth.

How do we adjust our sights to see these opportunities? I believe we must first step out of our comfort of contentment and mediocrity to seek the necessary information needed to explore the possibilities of creating and building wealth. Become financially literate and understand the value and workings of money and credit.

Dream big with purpose, drive, ambition, love, and determination. Have the right intentions and allow yourself to think outside the box; explore your imagination, and you can reach your dream while being accepted for who you are.

- Electronically Traded Fund (ETF). There are a lot of ETFs that invest in commodities (steel, oil, etc.), energy, real estate, stock indexes (S&P 500), currencies, bonds, and other assets. An ETF owns the underlying assets and then breaks that ownership up into shares. These shares are traded on a stock exchange by individual investors. The buying and selling of ETF shares does not change the underlying assets that are held. ETF prices are based on the market price, and are sold only in full shares.
- Value Stocks. These are stocks of established companies that have stable revenues, cash flows, and dividends that trade at a deal during volatile times in the market.

As with all investments, do your own research and come to an understanding that you are comfortable with before investing your money. Don't be afraid to seek professional financial advice and read as much as you can about investment vehicles that can work for you.

Stock trades are free these days at most online brokerages. But where and how your trade is filled can impact your purchase price, and "it all happens in a flash."

Step one: You click "Buy"

After you submit a trade, before it is routed to the next step, your brokerage firm will review your trade for certain factors. The size of your trade can influence where and how the order is filled and the price you pay.

Fractional orders or oversized orders (say, more than 10,000 shares), for instance, may be filled in multiple transactions. Some firms may scrutinize a trade for whether it could impact the stock's trading price. An exceptionally large order could drive the price of a stock up or down, and you don't want that.

Some firms also check to see that you have the cash or margin in your account to cover the trade; others may give you leeway to fund the account over the next two business days.

Step two: Routing

Your broker has a duty to deliver the best possible execution price to you for your trade, which means it must meet or beat the best price available in the market. To do so, it can choose to send your order to one of four venues.

Market makers, including firms such as Citadel and Virtu Financial, act like car dealers for buyers and sellers. These firms will pay a fraction of a penny for every share that your broker sends their way in a practice called "payment for order flow." Although some brokers don't accept payment for order flow, it's not necessarily a bad thing: in exchange for the order flow, the market maker also promises to beat your quote page. Say the current market price for XYZ stock is fifty dollars. The market maker may fill your order at $49.98 a share. That's price improvement.

Brokerages must disclose how much they receive in payment for order flow every year.

An exchange, such as NASDAQ or the New York Stock Exchange, can fill the order too. But the exchanges charge your broker roughly thirty cents for every one hundred shares traded. Doesn't sound like a lot, but every penny adds up.

Some brokers, but not all, may fill the trade from their own inventory. The broker makes money on the "spread"—the difference between the purchase price and the sale price.

Alternative systems are a last option. Most trades don't end up here. These systems match buyers with sellers. In some cases, there's little transparency. That's why they're called "dark pools."

$

Step three: Confirmation

You'll get a notification that the order was filled, at what price, and at what time. If the order was small (fractional) or oversized (10,000 shares or more) you might see multiple executions.

$

Wealth is the progressive mastering of matter by mind.

—Anonymous

PILLAR III POLITICS

Prison Is …

Prison is an unsolvable puzzle never meant to be put together, because it was created with pieces missing. Prison is an inconvenience on life and should be avoided by all means necessary.

Being introduced to the prison system at the tender infant stage of our lives from visiting incarcerated loved ones tends to take away the fear and abnormalities of incarceration, often mistaken as a rite of passage to manhood. No one wants to speak about how horrible prison is and the effects of its confinement on one's mental and physical health. Every day is met with the constant attempt to escape the hardships of being away from loved ones and the life a person would like to live.

The nights are long and filled with distress as the reality sets in; being caged up when the lights go out, there's no escaping the regrets of a person who can subject themselves to such conditions. You are awakened and moved throughout the day like cattle by a bell that rings for you to move from one activity to the next, as correction officers line up to make sure you stay the course in an orderly fashion, waiting to reprimand you for any action, like refusing the last direct order given. This is another way to make sure your stay of incarceration is a little longer, knowing the parole board frowns upon misconduct, no matter how small the infraction.

To visit with loved ones, we are both degraded and embarrassed to some degree for security's sake. Our visitors' hands are subjected to drug scans that usually read positive, because virtually all US currency is tainted (as the FBI has proven) but required for the vending machines in order for us to eat during the visit. And prisoners are stripped naked, down to our dignity, going out and coming in from the visit. How do you not go crazy?

Welcome to prison, DK3774. Where or to whom do you want your body sent?

Rosedale Ave.

Politics is the art of compromise. What's in it for me; what can I keep you from getting?

—**Anonymous**

An injustice anywhere is an injustice everywhere.

—Frederick Douglass

After the Civil War and the Emancipation Proclamation and the so-called "freedom" slaves were given, there was a program devised to enslave the Black man's mind. There was state legislation that intentionally made the US Constitution illegal for Black people to study, for fear that we might learn to demand the rights guaranteed therein. This was our introduction into politics and the system designed to keep us down, defeated, dependent, and inferior. It was simple: marginalize Black people so we don't count. Repress us so we don't achieve political or economic power. Confine us to permanent underclass status as servants and slaves to keep us from rising equal to or above the ruling white class.

When Grams spoke about politics, she spoke about a system designed for the demise of the Black man. The system she spoke about was incarceration. Grams would say, "It only takes a minute to get caught up in the system. It will take a lifetime to get out of!"

Why wouldn't she feel that way? Grams's husband, her son, and my father were all captured by the system, never to come up from under it. Her husband died while incarcerated at the State Correctional Institution in Pittsburgh (Western Penitentiary). Her son found himself in and out of jail. My father is still fighting to get out of prison, serving a life sentence after forty-three years.

I read in the book *Snitch* by Ethan Brown that incarceration rates are so high in the Black community that even middle- to upper-class Black men have some contact with the prison system. A June 2006 *Washington Post* poll found that even among Black men with college degrees and household incomes of $75,000 a year or more, six in ten said someone close to them had been murdered, and six in ten said a family member or close friend had been in jail or prison. This puts them in the same camp as working-class, less-educated Black men. It is the most profound crisis in Black American life since segregation.

That article was written seventeen years ago. Since then, things have gotten worse. Frustration, anger, despair, and mayhem are all ingredients used to make a human dirty bomb. As we choose to implode and explode on each other, the murder rates rise in our communities all over.

I was an eighteen-year-old kid walking into a den of wolves. The wolves were the homicide detectives. They smelled blood as soon as I decided to talk to them without a lawyer. Worst decision of my life. Although what I said was contrary to the evidence against me, it has made my path to freedom that much harder.

There I was with no clue about homicide charges and what I was facing. My family put some money together to retain an attorney for me. I had a crash course in law and legal matters. They gave me a speedy trial, which meant I was going to court in six months. I thought this was a good thing. Turns out it wasn't,

Hale St.

and I was left ill prepared. I learned that defense attorneys have an obligation to the courts first, because they are sworn officers of the courts.

The lawyer my family retained did little to no investigation into my case. He didn't seek any witnesses. I saw him a total of four times and called him a total of ten times on the phone. Not to mention, after every visit with him and every time I talked to him on the phone, my family was billed. This happened from February 1997 to July 1997. No witnesses, with an alibi defense from a female I was courting at the time and a character witness who was a teacher from school.

Barry's Market

The day before I was set to start trial, I had a last minute "strategy" meeting with my attorney. He started by saying there was an offer on the table and by law he had to present it to me. He continued talking, saying their offer was for me to implicate someone else as the shooter other than myself in my case. In turn, they would charge me with a lesser offense that carried a five- to ten-year sentence, and they would suspend the sentence so I wouldn't have to spend a day in prison.

That offer told me exactly what I knew the whole time or thought I knew. They didn't have a case against me. In my mind, I was coming home. The case was over. We wrapped up the "strategy" meeting. I couldn't wait to call my Grams and tell her they didn't have a case against me and why. I called and told her I just finished meeting with the attorney. I asked if she believed what they offered as a deal. Before I could say another word, she said, "You can't speak about what you don't know about."

I said, "That goes without saying, Grams. So, what are we talking about?"

"Nothing at all!" she said. Moving on, she asked, "Do you need anything?"

"Nah, I'm cool."

Grams said she would see me in court the next day and to put my armor of God on in prayer. "I love you, son." She wasn't trying to hear nothing. She was mad at the lawyer for bringing the offer. She told him she didn't pay him for that.

My trial was a circus of sorts. It lasted three days. The jury seemed to deliberate longer than the trial lasted. They came back with a guilty verdict of murder in the first degree after seven hours.

After my debacle of a trial, I didn't know what was next. My lawyer told me I was on my own after trial because my family couldn't afford to pay him for an appeal. I thought that was bold to say to an individual who just lost their life. My family was distraught; no one knew what to do. All we knew was, the next phase of this saga was an appeal, and wondered how we were going to pay for it.

This was my introduction to politics. I was playing a game without understanding what the stakes were my life. As I stated in the chapter about math, making bad decisions without taking into account the consequences or, worse yet, not caring about any consequences at all, leads to a lose-lose outcome.

I am still in pursuit of my freedom. I have been through the appeal process a total of six times. The district attorney explained to the courts that if I received a new trial, it would prejudice their case against me, because they don't have any evidence to try me again. I even tried to be resentenced as a juvenile three times, since I was eighteen years old when I was arrested. Pennsylvania has yet to consider eighteen-year-olds as juveniles. Although the law here says you have to be at least twenty-one years old to buy tobacco products, teenagers can get sentenced to life without parole or serve in the armed services of the United States. Interesting. Connecticut, Illinois, Massachusetts, Michigan, New York, San Francisco, and Washington State, to name a few, have changed their laws to consider eighteen- to twenty-year-olds as juveniles.

The justice system is just a part of the systematic machine working against us as a race in this great nation of the US of A. Here it is the twenty-first century, and we are still fighting for civil liberties. It is said "racism is as American as apple pie." In 2020, the gap between the civil rights era and the civil unrest of today finally bridged the generations together. Instead of being hung like strange fruit from trees, we were being shot to death while unarmed, or choked to death by hands or knees of white police officers and the so-called crusaders of morality who take the law into their own hands.

Enough is enough! Black and white people alike came together in a global protest against such hate and inhumane treatment of Black men and Black women. Groups such as Color of Change and Black Lives Matter put the establishment of America on notice. No more will Black people be an afterthought. There were going to be some historic changes made in the systemic racist machine that plagues our communities.

We find ourselves still fighting voter suppression and oppression in some form or fashion. The state of Pennsylvania elected its first Black lieutenant governor, and the city of Pittsburgh showed up and showed out to elect its first Black mayor. Those are big steps in the right direction. The saying goes, "Never judge a book by its cover." As Black men, we don't have the luxury. We are plagued with negative stereotypes of what and who we are. What I am always starts by way of where I come from. Who I am is defined by what I have or have not accomplished. Understanding this thought process of our white counterparts, we have to show there is more to us than where we come from and what we may have endured because of the roadblocks placed in front of us.

Politics are about how you are perceived through the eyes of others and how to form relationships. Grams would express the importance of how your first impression should be your best impression. It's not what you know. It's who you know. In our case, both are equally important. We can only get invited by what we know. Then we need validation from someone in position to bring us into the fold so we can sit at the table.

It's evident we have only scratched the surface. Here it is the twenty-first century, and we are still celebrating first African American milestones. As if we've been sitting around doing nothing. We just haven't been acknowledged, validated, and brought into the fold. We are a resilient, pioneering type of people. *We make our own way!*

post-gazette.com

A service of the **Pittsburgh Post-Gazette**®

False Confessions: Da' Ron Cox / Only evidence remaining against him is confession

Friday, September 01, 2006

By Cynthia Levy, Special to the Post-Gazette

In November 1996 Brian Roberts pointed an automatic weapon at a police officer and was arrested. He was carrying 34 rocks of crack cocaine. He walked free after telling police the gun and drugs belonged to Roland Cephas.

Mr. Cephas was busted and vowed retaliation.

Ten days later, as Mr. Roberts stood on Sterrett Street in Homewood, a man in a black coat, scull cap and blue jeans shot him twice, chased him into an alley, pumped two more bullets into him, pistol-whipped him and left him to die.

The officer who persuaded Mr. Roberts to snitch told homicide detectives that Mr. Cephas was a likely suspect. No one implicated Da'Ron Cox, 18, or even placed him at the scene.

Fourteen days later, a young man incarcerated at Shuman Juvenile Detention Center, in exchange for money and freedom, told police he saw Mr. Cox commit the murder. Police used the statement to extract a confession from the kid known on the streets as "Chicken."

Mr. Cox has said ever since that he didn't kill Mr. Roberts and never confessed. He is serving a life sentence.

The interrogation

Mr. Cox says he was interrogated from 7 p.m. until 1:30 a.m. without counsel while shackled to the ground. Police recorded only the final few minutes, so there is no record to confirm or refute Mr. Cox's account.

"I kept telling them I was with my girlfriend in Penn Hills and they kept telling me they knew I did it and that they had me red-handed," said Mr. Cox. His girlfriend said she spent Friday nights during that period with Mr. Cox but couldn't remember that specific evening.

City detectives Robert McCabe, now deceased, and Dennis Logan, now an investigator for the Allegheny County District Attorney's Office, took turns playing good cop, bad cop, Mr. Cox said.

Detective Logan refused to comment.

"They started telling me they knew I wasn't a violent person because they pulled my juvenile record and they knew I never carried a gun so [they told me] it would be real easy to get me off if I confessed," he said.

When Mr. Cox refused to admit the killing, he said, detectives told him they could make this into a "self-defense thing," charging him with manslaughter, which carries a minimum two-year sentence. He decided to cut his losses.

"When you live the lifestyle that I was living you become conditioned to do time. You know you'll eventually go to jail and I was just thinking two years and I'll put it behind me," he said.

Conflicting statements

The Shuman Center informant claimed he saw Mr. Cox shoot the victim at close range in the chest. In his "confession," Mr. Cox also told police he fired six shots into Mr. Robert's chest, but from a distance.

Mr. Roberts was shot in the back.

At the July 1997 trial, police denied manipulating the young Mr. Cox to get a confession. Detective McCabe could not account for the conflict between the physical evidence and the statements of both Mr. Cox and the informant.

On the witness stand, Mr. Cox denied involvement, claiming he confessed after hours of questioning because he was promised a short prison term if he did and was led to fear the death penalty if he didn't.

After a three-day trial, Mr. Cox was convicted and sentenced to life in prison without parole.

"When I heard the judge say I was guilty I was not surprised. There was a lady on the jury I made eye contact with. She nodded at me before they went to deliberate like everything would be OK, but when she came out crying, I just looked at my mom and said, 'That's how the cookie crumbles,' " said Cox.

Post-trial revelations

After the trial, several men signed affidavits stating that they knew Mr. Cox had not been at the murder scene and that Mr. Roberts was killed because of his dispute with Mr. Cephas. Mr. Cephas himself was murdered in 1997.

Allegheny County Common Pleas Judge Jeffrey Manning denied an appeal at that point.

Then another man signed an affidavit swearing that the Shuman Center informant, the only eyewitness against Mr. Cox, had actually been with him at the time of the killing and could not have seen anything. The informant was gunned down in 1999.

Since then, yet another man has sworn that he saw Mr. Cephas kill Mr. Roberts.

Ten years later, Mr. Cox remains the sole surviving suspect in this string of retaliatory street gang killings. He says he had nothing to do with Mr. Robert's death or any of the others. The only remaining evidence against him, he says, is his own alleged confession.

"I just hope that one day someone will see that the whole situation was not right and lets me out," he says.

Mr. Cox's attorney is preparing a final appeal to federal court.

Back

_____

Courage isn't having the strength to go on—it is going on when you don't have the strength.

—Napoleon Bonaparte

PILLAR IV RELIGION

Race St.

A man by his sin may waste himself, which is to waste that which on earth is most like God. This is man's greatest tragedy and God's heaviest grief.

—**A.W. Tozer**

Religion

For God has not given us a spirit of fear, but of power and love and of a sound mind.

—2 Timothy 1:7

Religion is salvation for the soul. God is love and wants us to enjoy life. We should all strive to establish a relationship with God and share His Word and how He is very tender in affection and merciful. We make God happy when we do good things, when we are of service to our fellow humans, and when we love each other as He has loved us. Grams came up in an era when pimps and con men turned to the pulpit to hustle. For that very reason she would not step foot into a church. She would get her Bible and hold church in her bedroom. Grams would speak about the power of faith and having a relationship with God.

Growing up, I attended different churches. I would come home and share my experiences. There wasn't much to it, since I was still trying to figure out how Christianity fit into my life. How do I go about having a relationship with God? My household wasn't religious. Although Grams shared her beliefs with me, I was allowed to seek my own understanding and spiritual path.

I was once invited to go to church with Black. He was a member of Mount Ararat Church. I went, and it turned out to be a positive, uplifting experience. Black and I had a big-brother-little-brother relationship. He helped me navigate through my growing pains and provided me insight on certain subjects. Black would challenge me to be different from my peers. Black proceeded to show me the way he started out with a booth at the farmers market and turned it into a storefront.

Church was his foundation, which put him in position to be the man he was. Black was striving to instill this in me. Mount Ararat Church had me. They had a come-as-you-are policy. The members were very welcoming. I started the process to get baptized, to become a member of the church; however, I fell off and so did my relationship with Black. Black had no room in his life for, the path I chose, which I understood. That's another relationship I couldn't repair. I was hurt too. Looking deeply within, I had to reevaluate my existence. I feel, at that time, that existing was all I was doing.

I've spent the better part of my incarceration seeking redemption and striving to mend relationships. Some people I haven't had an opportunity to speak with. To others I have been able to extend my apologies. I was thankful they were receptive and forgiving. There were some not so receptive and forgiving. I understand. I too had to forgive people I may have felt wronged me, even if they didn't ask or care one way or the other. I did it for me; I couldn't carry the weight of what I felt others didn't do for me. It would have been an anchor that was sure to drag me down and hold me in a dark and lonely place. I learned *nobody* owes you anything.

I haven't been the best person, friend, or cousin. I came up short more than I would like to admit. How could I hold others to a standard I didn't uphold myself? That's why I had to forgive, as I too sought forgiveness for my past indiscretions on this journey to solidify and strengthen my personal relationship with God. God has been a major factor in my perseverance during these years of incarceration. My faith has been tested. There were many days of doubt, but in those moments, God blessed me with His presence. That doesn't mean my pain or trouble went away, but there was a comfort and an assurance that everything would work out for the better.

Grams would quote Hebrews 11:1: "Now faith is the substance of things hoped for, the evidence of things not seen."

I was unsure of how I was going to pay for an appeal. My Aunt Lump was working for a man named Richard at the time. He was a tech consultant. My aunt asked him if he could help the family in any way to get me home. His response was, "I don't know anything about the law. What can I do?" She asked if he could at least read the case. He looked, with no clue of what he was reading. As he continued to read, though, the case opened up to him. He saw the inconsistencies and how contrary they were to the physical evidence.

My first conversation with Richard while I was still at SCI Camp Hill. He was straightforward and asked would I be willing to take a lie detector test before he signed on to help me. I said yes. Unbeknownst to me, this was a test. If I had said no, he would have thought I had something to hide. He said, "I don't know what I can do. I will help the best I can."

During my first round of appeals I had a court-appointed lawyer for my direct appeal. At the time, appeal lawyers were exempt from due diligence and effective counseling. That's no longer true, thanks to a case that came down in 2021, *Commonwealth v. Bradley*, that holds appeal counsel accountable for ineffective counsel. I learned that through the appeal process, there is a clock that must be managed to take your appeal to the federal courts. In my case, the lawyer who represented me for my appeal was just a figurehead. The burden was on me. The first round was not in my favor.

Richard and I had to change strategies. Richard put his money and time into action. I reached out to home, and home reached back in a major way. I received help from people all over. These folks held me up. They were talking to potential witnesses, showing up to my hearings, helping me file paperwork, and sending me cases. There were writing sessions to the judge and district attorney's office(s) to reopen my case. Placing a letter or story about my character in an article in the Pittsburgh *Post-Gazette*. Donating to my legal fund, passing out pamphlets, and wearing "Free Da'Ron" T-shirts.

I was provided a circle of camaraderie and support assuring me I wasn't in this fight alone. Richard got the first paid appeal attorney. A couple of people stepped up and made it possible for me to receive the first of two evidentiary hearings. My attorney ended up filing two inconsistent affidavits for one of the two individuals who stepped up for me. I asked, "Why? You made it appear as if he is lying." I explained to my attorney that he was suppose to have the individual elaborate once we were at court.

This imbecile of an attorney said, "Don't worry. I am going to treat him as a hostile witness." That made no sense, being he was willing to come to court and testify on my behalf. I told this attorney I felt he was helping the DA keep me in prison. Richard wanted to see how it played out.

I was scheduled an evidentiary hearing, and to the DA's surprise both witnesses showed up and were ready to speak on my behalf. The DA requested a postponement because he was unprepared and thought they were going to be no-shows. The judge granted his request and rescheduled another hearing within thirty days.

I wasn't feeling the double affidavit situation. However, I was hopeful of what was to come at the next evidentiary hearing. The night before my evidentiary hearing, one of the witnesses was in a car accident that had a fatality. Didn't know who. Just that the witness was in the car.

Once again, I was at the mercy of the courts. No way was the witness making it to court. The other witness was available because he was already in the Allegheny County Jail. My attorney requested a postponement until we could get an idea of what was going on. All we knew was there'd been an accident with a fatality.

The judge denied our request for a postponement. We proceeded to put forth our best argument with the one witness.

I asked the attorney, along with Richard, what options I had. This guy had no clue. I couldn't process anything that was going on. I got back to the Allegheny County Jail feeling like I couldn't catch a break. My people were caught up in their own emotions. I still didn't know what happened or how; I kept hearing it was an accident.

Within the next two weeks I received the news that my appeal was denied. Back to the drawing board. I had to find a way to get home.

God answered my prayer. New evidence became available from a new witness. I got my attorney into action. He interviewed the witness and put together an affidavit. The witness signed the affidavit and got it notarized.

At that time, you had sixty days to file newly discovered evidence (now you have up to a year).

Both Richard and I pressured the attorney to file this new discovery of evidence. He assured us he was on it, and everything was on schedule. What did he do? He let the sixty days lapse. I went at him. He was trying to tell me the law. I told him that's nonsense. The law at the time said you had sixty days from the time you learned of the newly discovered evidence to file an appeal, not from the time the affidavit is signed and notarized.

We fired him right there. Now we were in search of a new attorney. We found one, and he had to file an extension to get caught up with the case and correct what the last attorney did. He was on it, and I received an evidentiary hearing for the newly discovered evidence. My last attorney was called to testify and explain his actions. When this guy said he thought the sixty days started from the time the affidavit was signed, both the judge and the DA started laughing. I couldn't help but think he was working with them.

Twice I had everything I needed to present my case and get the outcome I'd been praying for, only to have the very person who was supposed to represent my best interests intentionally do an ineffective job.

By this time, I had exhausted all my appeals. Without any new or exculpatory evidence, I didn't have a chance. Richard had been on the radio talking about my case, passing out pamphlets, and he even held a rally. The Point Park College Innocence project took interest in my case. They did a national story in the

Pittsburgh *Post-Gazette* about my case. Some information surfaced that there was exculpatory evidence in my initial police file. Point Park College initiated the process to retrieve the evidence, but they were denied. Richard had the attorney try as well; he was denied. I filed a Right to Know Act petition; I too was denied. Everyone was stumped at this point, because it wasn't adding up. The source of the information wanted to stay anonymous out of fear of losing their pension.

Richard reached out to Temple University, who also has an innocence project. I filled out the necessary forms and waited to be contacted. Temple's innocence project had four stages. If you made it to the fourth stage, they would provide a legal team to work on your case. I made it to the third stage. Since I didn't have any new or exculpatory evidence they couldn't help me.

In stepped a woman of faith. I call her God's pit bull. She started turning over every stone to get to the bottom of things. She caused a wave of uneasiness in downtown Pittsburgh. She was persistent, but without that key evidence, even her unyielding tenacity was met with an abrupt stop.

As I went back to the drawing board, an elder from home reached out, offering to help me with commutation. He got all the information I needed. He devised a plan how he was going to present me to the board of pardons. He made the necessary contacts. I wrote about my accomplishments, who I had become, and what I intended to do upon my release from incarceration, only to find out a person serving a life sentence has to have at least twenty years in before being considered for commutation. I had eighteen years in.

It's not for a lack of effort or support that I haven't overturned my conviction. God continues to bless me with His presence to assure me He is my refuge. I am blessed to have a great support team who tirelessly work with me to get me home. Richard and I are still in the trenches, along with countless others who have helped and continue to help me by writing letters to the board of pardons, giving me the support of the community in hopes that I can receive commutation.

The people at home who continue to breathe life into me, holding me up in thought and prayer. Those who inquire about my well-being, taking the time to accept my calls and visit me. Those who encouraged me to write this book. My big sis, who helped me with the process to put my best work forward. My little brother, who put me in position to fulfill my entrepreneurial aspirations by selling dogs, helping me print T-shirts to help fund the publishing of my book. Those who bought a T-shirt to help me get a win. My moms for selling the T-shirts at work. Drewpa said, "He believed in me" and attached his horse to my cart and told me to get to it.

Then God placed an angel in my life at a time when I was feeling like I was drowning. I needed a win badly. I was questioning the purpose of my existence. The walls were closing in, and I felt inadequate. I was given a lifeline and a whole new outlook on life.

My angel whispered to me, "The *win* is coming. Don't let the *when* worry you."

The Angel who came into my life helped me cross the finish line, taking on the task of finding a publisher and making sure the business of the book was handled professionally. All the while showing me what it looks like and feels like to have a true partner and a love that is for me, with me, and about me unconditionally.

Believing in me, wanting me to achieve success, taking this journey with me, and being my biggest supporter. My Angel, I love you and appreciate you more than you will ever know.

Thanks to my little sis for making sure I have a relationship with my nieces and nephew.

Most important, keeping our relationship strong. To my baby girl, know that Ba Ba loves you. Know your worth and never settle.

I say this to say I couldn't do anything without the love and support of so many who after twenty-six years are still there for me, praying for that day when I can walk as a free man. I once was a child but am now a man of a village that is and will always be my home, Homewood-Brushton, Pennsylvania. I can't say "thank you" enough. I hope to make you proud.

To those who were and are my biggest doubters and naysayers: as Hov would say, "They hate when we become more than what they expected."

There are people I lost who came through for me in the darkest time of my life. Words cannot express my gratitude and appreciation for their loyalty. The bulletproof love, support, and sacrifice to hold me up, standing with me even in my absence. I carry them with me. You find out who your true people are when you're upstate bleedin'.

In implementing the Four Pillars, I have come to learn that *Education* puts me in the best position to succeed in life. *Math* allows me to look at a problem in its entirety to make the most rational decision, plus keeps me financially responsible, always working toward building wealth. In understanding *Politics*, I've learned it is a system that is supposed to protect the interests of the people no matter a person's socioeconomic background, to allow them a fair and equal opportunity to share in the pursuit of happiness in the country we call home. A home where *Religion* provides structure based upon something greater than oneself, a faith from which you can find comfort and strength in knowing that, at your weakest and darkest times, God is there to see you through, turning tribulation into a blessing that can change your life in a way that surpasses your wildest dreams of accomplishments.

Overcoming Adversity

Rejoicing in hope, patient in tribulation, continuing steadfastly in prayer.

—Romans 12:12

Victory is your heritage in Christ. God is with you, and you will have great success in all things. Walk blameless and upright before God, and He will be your shield and give you the victory over any adversity you face.

Through Christ's life, death, and resurrection you have attained righteousness and strength to achieve great things. I declare that you will remain steadfast, immovable, always abounding in the work of the Lord, knowing that your labor is not in vain. Any evil words or destructive actions formed against you will be powerless and shall fall away.

God will take you from strength to strength and from triumph to triumph, for whatever is born of God is victorious over the world. Give thanks to God who promises to preserve you, deliver you, and give you the victory in all things.

PHOTO GALLERY

My "Gram's" Evelyn Cox worked for the board of education as a security guard for 30+years.

My "Moms" Robyn Cox and me at my graduation ceremony at Bethesda Church Head Start Program.

My "Pops" Ronald Smith and me on a visit at Western Penitentiary.

On a Rolling Skating field trip with Schenley High School.

In my fur coat and hat headed to Sunday night skating at Spinning Wheels.

My Sister Evony and my nieces Milana, My'Elle, and my nephew DALC.

Chiccen 95

Chiccen 96

My Gram's and my Mom's dancing at a cabaret at the Coliseum.

MY HEARTBEAT

Where do I begin?

When you stand with the blessings of your mother and God, it matters not who stands against you.

—Yoruba proverb

Where do I begin to express my ultimate appreciation for the person who has made the ultimate sacrifice to give me life? I start by saying thank you. Surely I owe her more. She, who was just a child herself, made a vow to give her life in order for her son to have the best life she could provide, loving him unconditionally. She did not know the task that awaited her and how hard it would become, especially when my father was taken away for a lifetime stay in the penitentiary. You made no excuses and pushed forward anyway. You made sure I knew my father's love, taking me to visit him, and accepting his collect calls. Showing me despite his circumstances he was a good man.

Where do I begin to express my ultimate appreciation?

Growing up, we bonded as siblings more than mother and son. So much so, you told me to call you Robyn. You would fight with me over the toy in the cereal box and wrestle with me so I could be able to protect myself just as my father did. Teaching me the importance of being kind, but not letting anyone take advantage of me.

Where do I begin to express my ultimate appreciation?

My taste in music and fashion are all you. You would hold me and sing "Thanks" by Cheryl Pepsii Riley. You gave me my sense of style. Taking me to my first concert. Fresh Fest '85, you had me fresh 2 def in a Puma tracksuit, suede Puma tennis shoes with fat shoestrings, a Kangol bucket hat, and Cazel glasses. Then you turned around and put me in some wingtips, blue jeans creased and cuffed, with a Polo buttondown. I can see how I was always your little old man.

Where do I begin to express my ultimate appreciation?

You taught me the art of chivalry. You taught me having multiple women doesn't make a man, but the way you treat a woman and respect a woman does. Respect goes both ways, you said, and be mindful of the games women play. Remembering how you taught me to fast dance, showing me it's okay to let a woman lead; telling me not to be a man intimidated by a woman who is confident in herself.

Uplifting

Where do I begin to express my ultimate appreciation for the person who has made the ultimate sacrifice to give me life? I start by saying thank you. Surely, I owe you more, for you carried me for nine months and nine years, allowing me to explore my curiosities while picking me up when I fell short, as you continued to stand by me and stand with me, love unwavering. Telling me how proud you are of the man I have become. This amazing woman is Moms!

I love you, Moms.

Dream like you never seen obstacles.

—J. Cole

My Heartbeat

All that I got is you and I'm so thankful we made it through.

—Ghostface Killa feat. Mary J. Blige

I am my grandmother's son. From the moment Moms gave birth to me, our bond was solidified. Grams named me Chiccen. She said I looked like a little bird. Moms said it was because all she ate was chicken wings while she was pregnant with me. I was born and raised in Homewood-Brushton, Pennsylvania. I grew up and lived at 7322 Kelly Street my whole life. I was nurtured by Grams and Moms, reared by my community. I once asked Grams about our family tree. She said, "I don't have a tree. But I got a few leaves."

Because I was an only child, Homewood became my extended family. When I left my house, I was always home no matter where I went in the community. Homewood was full of culture, from the Harambee Festival to the talent shows and plays held at the Homewood-Brushton Carnegie Library Auditorium, and the Friday night parties and concerts at the Coliseum. What was being taught at home was reinforced by the elders of the community, and there were expectations regarding my conduct. The care, concern, and love extended throughout the community, from Little League sports to after-school education programs at the YMCA.

The Coliseum used to have Thursday night roller skating for adults, which was Moms's favorite outing. Grams would take me up there and sneak me in the side door so I could skate a song with Moms before I went to bed. The best times were Saturday afternoons at the Coliseum, when Moms, Grams, and I would skate together. Three generations; truly a family affair.

Because Grams worked in the schools, I was able to go on roller skating field trips with Reizenstein Middle School and Schenley High School students. Then I got turned on to Spinning Wheels on Sunday nights. I would beg Moms to go with her. I was still in elementary school. As long as I would get up for school Monday morning, I could go. Anybody who was somebody in the city was there. After Spinning Wheels, Oakland was like the after-party.

I got a lot of my swag from those Sunday nights at Spinning Wheels. The beginning of my D-Boi aspirations. I was like a sponge. Spinning Wheels is the reason why I asked for and received a fur coat at the age of ten. I didn't want toys.

Before baseball consumed my summers, Grams and I would be on the go. She kept me in programs and summer camps. There were Saturday morning computer classes at the Kingsley Center and Jewish summer camps. At one point I thought I was Jewish, eating bagels and lox, celebrating Hanukkah, playing little dreidel games, and lighting a menorah. Grams would even put the Star of David in my bedroom window. I asked when was I having a bar mitzvah. She politely corrected me and said it's about the experience, learning and respecting another culture. We would also go visit her friends who lived in Shadyside and on the Northside. She wanted me to see how the other half lived, wanting me to feel comfortable socializing with them.

Joy

When I started playing baseball, that's all I wanted to do. Grams was my biggest fan. She was at every game and received a trophy for attendance. My first game I hit a triple. As I was running the bases, rounding second base into third, my coach was telling me to slide. I said, "I'm not sliding. I have to walk home. I'm not getting dirty."

My coach said, "It's part of the game, Chiccen." All I was worried about was being dirty walking home. Not cool!

I broke my left arm by getting hit by a fastball pitch; fractured my right arm getting hit by a bat. I see why they named me Chiccen. My arms snapped like chicken bones. It's safe to say I was committed after that. Grams would practice fielding drills with me behind Baxter School, throwing the ball in the air for fly balls, on the ground for grounders, plus throwing and catching exercises. You couldn't tell me I wasn't going to be the next Ozzie "The Wiz" Smith, minus the backflips. I even got traded to the Cardinals from the Pirates.

As sweet as my Grams could be, she was just as stern. I had to be feeling myself one day and decided I was going to talk back to her. She punched me in my chest, knocking me up against the door. As I slid down the door to the floor holding my chest, she said, "Now get out of my face." I'm thinking, *You punched me. You get out of* my *face.* I didn't dare say it, though. I just got up holding my chest and went to my room.

She had a way of bringing me back to reality if I was feeling myself too much. Growing up I had buckteeth. They were a part of me, and I rocked them as such. Moms told me I had to get braces. I didn't want them.

Back then I took pride in how I walked out of my house. I had to be right, from head to foot. Every day was an event for me, and I had to put on. Grams said, "Don't tell him nothing. When he gets older, and he's dressed to the nines trying to bag a skirt, when he goes to open his mouth, and the girl walks away because his teeth greet her first, he's going to wish he had those braces then." Moms made the orthodontist appointment for the following week. I got those braces.

There's a certain pride that comes with growing up in Homewood-Brushton, Pennsylvania. Sometimes one can get lost in that pride, as the reputation tends to proceed itself. I embody Homewood through and through; going out wit' a bang—ready to bang out! I pledged my allegiance to CIP. I am a blue flag patriot. Community Revolution in Progress. When you live a certain life and you're from a certain area, it ain't on you sometimes, it's in you.

In pledging my allegiance, I alienated myself from Grams, the very person who made a way for me to have options to succeed. At this time, Grams would leave letters around the house for me to read because she didn't know how to talk to me anymore. The letters warned me about the choices I was making.

Grams told me I couldn't burn the candle on both ends, and that the world was bigger than the corners and cuts of Homewood. One letter asked where my self-respect was and when I became a follower. I still think of that letter, because at that point she didn't recognize her grandson. She was hurt and disappointed in who I was becoming, for who I had become. I remember one day, when I was signing in for the first day of school. The father of a friend of mine saw the name I signed, looked up, and said, "Chiccen?" He didn't recognize me.

Looking into how I was carrying myself, I can understand. I had lost myself. What was perceived as one thing got lost in translation. We were meant to be a brotherhood with purpose to protect the community and put order into a lawless lifestyle. I thought there was a right way to do wrong. I am aware of the asininity in that thought process. Instead, gangbangin' was steeped in violence and destroyed the very foundation paved by the elders who passed the torch to us to carry on the traditions that made Homewood special. With that very torch we burned the neighborhood down to the point it's not safe for us to call it home anymore. Only in name can I say, "I'm from Homewood." We chose to live somewhere else.

We have become numb to our destructive ways and accustomed to our destructive thought patterns, allowing the bottom to become our norm. More often than not, many will give a selfish response. In the end, "I" is all that matters. In the end you will lose, and there's no breakeven point or getting ahead. Too many gone and too many losses. It can't be for nothing. Where's the starting line to begin to live? Or are we content with being expendable?

I am not taking shots or pointing fingers. I am not exempt from contributing to the very cause of the destruction that plagues our community. I ask, do we want better for ourselves? We can never have what we are unwilling to pursue!

As I sit here twenty-six years into my incarceration, my purpose in writing this book is not to explore a life that could have been, or, more accurately, a life that should have been. My intent is to share the story of a young man who was groomed for success while coming of age in a neighborhood infamous for gangs, violence, and drugs, all too often ignoring the wisdom of his grams and elders, consistently making bad decisions that, ultimately, led to having my freedom taken forever.

All across this country there are thousands of young men growing up in treacherous environments, where they're just trying to make it home while ducking the steady rhythm of gunshots and the allure of being in the mud-moving work. Many teenagers face the difficult choice between hood life and the daunting prospect of pursuing a more promising future beyond their confined space of comfort.

I share the wisdom of Grams in hope that somewhere a young man will read my words and see the folly of entering life in the streets. Recognizing that with focus, perseverance, and making the right decisions, there is an exciting world out there in which one can build a rich, fulfilling life.

Grams is a phenomenal, caring, selfless, kind, strong, resilient, opinionated at times, loving, and personable person, on top of being an intelligent and great woman.

Grams, ever since 12:01 a.m. on May 31, 1978, you held me, never letting me go. You told me to promise that I will always remember your *whole* feelings about everything. Especially your unconditional love for me, what we are to each other, and how we are about each other. No one can take that away from us.

It is said, "You can tell the value of a man by the way he carries himself." My greatest accomplishment to date was restoring my self-respect. I was able to express my appreciation and gratitude for Grams's unyielding devotion to my life. I stand not broken but a man with purpose, a man of substance, character, integrity, and humility, earning the honor of carrying Grams's legacy.

My heartbeat, thank you for loving me unconditionally, providing a solid foundation for me to build upon to become a good person and a great man with the odds stacked against me. A win-win scenario.

"Success is to be measured not so much by the position reached in life, as by the obstacles overcome while trying to succeed." There are no truer words than those spoken by Booker T. Washington. More important than one man's life is order. There's no room to be average and no excuse not to be great.

Marcus Garvey said, "Life is an important function. It was given for the sole purpose of expression, man should have a purpose and that purpose he should always keep in view, with the hope of achieving it in the fullest satisfaction to himself. Be not aimless, drifting and floating with the tide that doesn't go your way. To find your purpose, you must search yourself and with the knowledge of what is good and what is bad, select your course, steering toward the particular object of your dream or desire."

Now the world can embody your wisdom too!

With love
Your begotten son
Da'Ron Cox

How Fulfillment Unfolds

- Admire, respect, and trust yourself.

- Achieve personal unity of heart and mind.

- Maintain your body.

- Acquire knowledge; learn truth.

- Discover and use your personal talents; find your proper place.

- Share what you learn with others; help others.

- Think positively.

- Be free of fear.

- Eliminate worry.

- Be poised.

- Make, have, and keep good friends.

- Plan carefully; prepare purposefully; proceed positively; pursue persistently.

- See the invisible; feel the intangible; achieve the impossible.

- Focus + Courage + Willingness to Work = Miracles

- Do the best you can where you are with what you have.

- Always give thanks for everything you have.

- When in doubt, pray.

When I was a child, I spoke as a child, I understood as a child, I thought as a child; but when I became a man, I put away childish things. For now we see in a mirror, dimly, but then face to face. Now I know in part, but then I shall know just as I also am known.

And now abide faith, hope, love, these three; but the greatest of these is love.

—I Corinthians 13:11–13

Praise

August 6 2014

Dear Son,

I've been where you are now in a
mental frame of mind, in 1968 I came in from
being out all night, looked around my apt, and it
wasn't as it should be and less what im capable of.
         I left my Children, in the door way to
fend for themselves, and my neighbors said my children
handled it real well, however my neighbors looked
out for them. They wern't babies at the time. I
left went to Cleveland and stayed with my uncle
and his wife.
         I made it clean to my uncle my purpose
wasn't to Party and be treated like I was on
Some vacation trip. I was there to get my head
in order, and being in a positive atmosphere its
exactly what I did. I Stayed one week and
When I returned home, I thanked my children
for how well they acted. After that I painted
my whole apt white, made all Black Curtains
by hand for my windows, My kitchen floor was
Zebra, my kitchen table was from the Goodwill,
it was a Picnic table from Some Park, it had
wax all over it, I turned the boards over and
painted them Black.
         The living room furniture was
Black trimed in Zebra and end table were connected
to the end of the couch and the carpet was Red.
aside from doing a different atmosphere in the

ef: 4348299 pg 91 of 94 for DARON COX

58

I went to school from 2:PM to 10:PM for Cosmotology and finished, and my children acted just like you acted when I wasn't home, they had people in and out, but I was determind to finish school and move up in life.

I got $85.00 every two weeks from Welfare my rent was $45.00 a month, and when the food stamps came out, we had to pay half before we could get them.

In 1972 my children came in from school and I was Packed to move, they said mom are we moving I said Yes, they ask me to where, I said I have no idea. I stayed Packed. I got a Job in 1972 Working for the Board of Education breaking up fights, I made $315.00 a month, I considered myself rich. I was 34 yrs old and I stayed untill I was 70 yrs, that was 35 yrs and I was the last Security left, I was an Original.

I moved in this house in 1974 and im still here, it's 40 yrs. My Children were never moved from house to house, they only lived two Places Projects for ten years and here.

The purpose of telling you this is, I left out the abuse I experinced at home and my marriage, I left out all the obstricles I experinced, but I never gave up. I was Kicked Throwed and Sculed, but I never fell.

Getting back to the Purpose of this letter, is to try and let You Know no matter where You are, there are always going to be obsticles. God willing You will be given a chance to be in a more Positive atmosphere and excel and accomplish everything You've PrePared yourself to do and be.

In the meantime continue to learn and use Your Pain and suffering to Your advantage. I was 40 Yrs old when You were born 12:01 a.m in 1978, im 76 Yrs old now and im still holding You in my heart.

I don't belive man will be how You get Free, I belive God has a Plan for you, and when You do get out You'll be free of the ties that caused you, Your Pain and suffering. I want to be Right.

Faith is the Subtance of things Hope for, The Evidence of things Not Seen

Love Ya! man
GRams

INDEX

Printed in the United States
by Baker & Taylor Publisher Services